Mother Wonderful's

Profusely Illustrated Guide to
the Proper Preparation of

Chicken Soup

Mother Wonderful's
Profusely Illustrated Guide to
the Proper Preparation of
Chicken Soup

Myra Chanin

A Dell Trade Paperback

A DELL TRADE PAPERBACK
Published by
Dell Publishing
a division of
Bantam Doubleday Dell Publishing Group, Inc.
1540 Broadway
New York, New York 10036

The trademark Dell® is registered in the U.S. Patent and Trademark Office.

ISBN: 0-440-50814-2

Printed in the United States of America

Published simultaneously in Canada

May 1997

10 9 8 7 6 5 4 3 2 1

hwk

For my mother, Sylvia ("Tsuni") Daskill, who was truly wonderful and frequently difficult, with eternal love and gratitude for setting such high standards for her daughter in food and in life.

Tsuni, wherever you may be, I hope you're pleased to have become an enduring classic, even though you never planned to become immortal by holding a chicken by its feet.

$\mathcal{E}$ARLY ONE MORNING . . .
when you know your daughter is having a busy day,
call your daughter and say you're catching cold.

Ask if she can spare a few minutes to drive you to a kosher butcher
so you can buy a chicken with feet for soup.

Everybody knows
chicken soup
is the best defense
against germs.

*R*emind her how quickly a cold can turn into double pneumonia, which everybody knows is the number one killer of senior citizens.

$\mathcal{W}$hen your daughter suggests you call the doctor because she has to deliver her new book to her editor by 4:00 P.M., happen to mention that your sister Becky's daughter, Sarah, the CPA, the partner in a Big Ten accounting firm, paid more taxes last year than most writers make in a lifetime. But when Becky sneezes, the IRS waits.

Wait outside in the cold
for your daughter.
When she drives up,
lean on your cane and . . .

. . . cough into your handkerchief.
Remember, you don't want to spread germs, just guilt.

$\mathcal{W}$hen you arrive at the butcher shop,
greet the owner as if he were your favorite brother,
rather than a person who intends to sell you a defective chicken.

Pretend to consider the chickens the butcher displays.
Pay no mind to claims of quality and freshness.

Everybody knows butchers hide their prime pullets
"in the back" for their favorites.

$\mathcal{B}$ide your time. Concentrate.
Wait patiently until the telephone rings.
The butcher will be distracted and stop watching you.

$\mathcal{W}$hile the butcher is talking on the phone
to another "wonderful" customer,
drop your cane and leap into the back.

$\mathcal{F}$ling open the door to the walk-in box . . .

. . . and return triumphant with a selection worthy of you.

$\mathcal{F}$ollow the butcher into the back,
and stare at him while he singes
the pinfeathers off your bird.

He could switch your selection
with a regular chicken
should your eyes even blink.

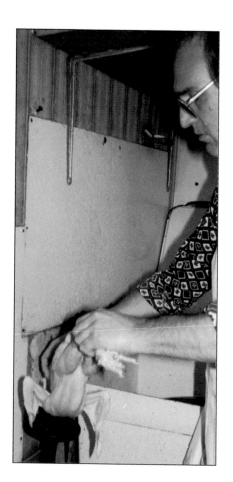

$\mathcal{T}$ell the butcher to include a few extra feet to give body to the soup.

If he says he has no extra feet, tell him to cut them off someone else's chicken.

$\mathcal{A}$sk your daughter
if she can spare a few more minutes
so you can pick up a few fresh vegetables to flavor the soup.

When she agrees, direct her to a market on the other side of town.

Spend at least forty minutes selecting two perfect carrots . . .

. . . the right parsley root, a fresh onion, and a small, crisp celery heart.

Everybody knows they hide the best vegetables
on the bottom of the pile.

$\mathcal{L}$et fourteen old folks step ahead of you in the checkout line.

Tell your daughter that a *mensch* is never in such a hurry
that she doesn't have time to be a little considerate
of working people who have to buy food
for their families during lunch hour.

$\mathcal{D}$uring the ride home complain that your kitchen is tiny and all your pots are chipped.

Ask your daughter if you could make soup at her house.
Ask her to stop at your building so you can pick up a clean work dress.

*R*eturn carrying your favorite chipped pot.

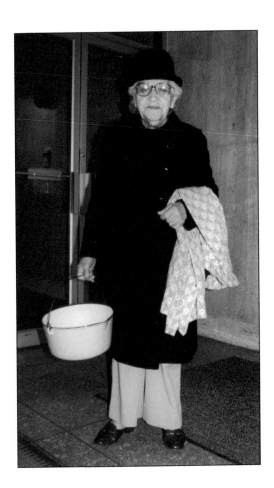

$\mathcal{T}$ell your daughter you are going upstairs to change your clothes.

Instead make the beds.

Pick up all the books and magazines lying open in the bedrooms. Stack them in a neat pile with the titles facing the wall so your daughter's family can't find what they were reading.

$\mathcal{V}$acuum the rugs
while your daughter attempts
to talk on the telephone.

Interrupt her conversation
to show her how nice the house
looks now.

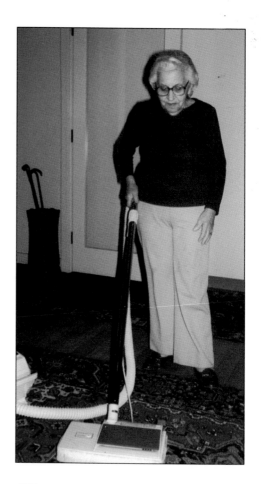

$\mathcal{R}$ecite an obscure Russian proverb that says it only takes a few minutes a day to turn a hovel into a palace

. . . and vice versa.

When your daughter screams at you, innocently ask how you offended her. Repeat the proverb in a benign voice. Skip the vice versa.

Sigh and limp into the kitchen.

Place the cut-up chicken in one bowl.
Place the feet in another bowl.
They are dirtier.

Start to prepare the soup.

Pour some boiling water on the chicken parts.
Pour twice as much boiling water on the feet.

Rinse the boiling water off the chicken parts.

Scrape the top layer of skin with a sharp knife to remove blemishes that eluded the butcher.

Rinse the feet three times.

With a different knife peel the top layer of skin from the feet.

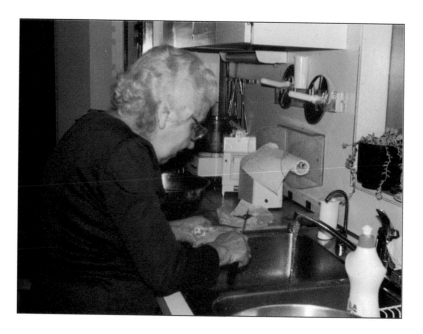

Rinse the chicken parts again because you touched them. Transfer them to a new, clean metal bowl.

$\mathcal{W}$ash your hands before and after you touch anything.

If you can't remember whether you rinsed something off, rinse it again to be safe.

Avoid adding germs to your soup.

Put the rinsed chicken parts in the bottom of your rinsed chipped pot.
Rinse the feet one last time, and place them on top.

Pour fresh boiling water into the pot.

*R*inse everything once more, including the vegetables.
Add the vegetables and a little salt to the pot.
Worry whether the salt is clean.

Let the contents simmer, lifting the lid every twenty-two seconds
to skim off anything that looks suspicious.

Check the progress of the soup by placing your palm
over the simmering liquid.

Scald the flesh of your inner arm by letting it brush against
the rim of the pot.

A second-degree burn is a small price to pay for good health.

$\mathcal{W}$hen no one is looking, put on a pot of rice.
Your grandson loves soup with rice.

Also cook a pot of noodles.
Your son-in-law loves soup with noodles.

$\mathcal{W}$hen you think the soup is ready, taste it.

$\mathcal{L}$et your grandson taste it.

$\mathcal{L}$et your son-in-law taste it.

*M*ake your daughter taste it.

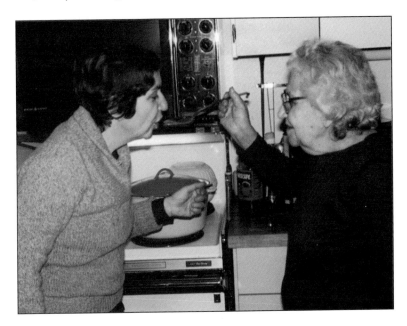

$\mathcal{A}$fter they all agree that this is absolutely the best soup they have ever eaten, taste it again yourself.

Wait forty-three seconds, and ask if they are *sure* the soup is all right.

Wrap up the beef Wellington your daughter prepared for her family's dinner, and put it in the freezer.

Set out bowls, and serve everyone soup.

When they ask why you aren't joining them, tell them you'll eat after you finish cleaning the kitchen.

Stand over the table with a ladle in your hand to refill bowls.

When you are not serving soup, cut up the cooked chicken meat and make chicken salad.

Your son-in-law loves your chicken salad.

Pour one-half cup of the soup into a tiny plastic container for yourself.

Place your chipped pot with the rest of the soup in the front of your daughter's refrigerator, near the chicken salad, so her family can find it when they are hungry again.

$\mathcal{D}$on your coat and hat,
and insist on walking back to
your apartment unescorted
in the dark.

Tell your grandson
—who loves chicken soup—
that there's more soup
in the refrigerator.

Tell your son-in-law
—who loves chicken salad—
that there's chicken salad
in the refrigerator.

Tell your daughter
it's nobody's fault that things
are different nowadays and
people are too busy
with their "careers" to ever
serve their families anything
but canned soup.

$\mathcal{T}$hat's why you're only taking a half cup of soup
home with you in a plastic container
and leaving the rest for them.

For you, fresh chicken soup is no big deal.
You can make it anytime.

$\mathcal{A}$s soon as you arrive home, call your sister, Becky.

Report that you woke up with the sniffles and when your
daughter called you, as she does every morning
to find out if you had a stroke during the night,
she could tell that everything wasn't hotsy-totsy.

She forgot all about the deadline on her new book,
which everybody says will be a runaway best-seller,
and rushed right over to see how you felt.

She even insisted on driving you to the kosher butcher
to buy a chicken so you could make some soup.

$\mathcal{E}$verybody knows there aren't many daughters as devoted as that around nowadays.

When Becky cuts the conversation short,
heat up the container of soup you brought home with you,
and savor every spoonful.

Tsuni's Golden Chicken Soup

EQUIPMENT

1 8-quart kettle or soup pot with a tight-fitting lid, preferably rescued from the old country and brought in steerage to America

INGREDIENTS

1 large kosher hen (5 to 6 pounds), with feet (if your butcher can't provide a stewing hen that large, add chicken parts to the one he gives you until you have 6 pounds of chicken)
6 to 8 extra chicken feet
Lots of boiling water for cleaning chicken
3 quarts boiling water
1 large carrot (about 10 ounces), cut into 3 big chunks
1 large onion (about 10 ounces), peeled and left whole
3 crisp celery stalks, cut into 3-inch pieces
1 entire scallion, including greens
1 large parsley root with greens attached (about 4 ounces), peeled and cut in half lengthwise

About 1 ounce fresh dill, tied together for easy removal when soup is finished
1 tablespoon kosher salt
¼ teaspoon white pepper

PREPARATION

Have your butcher cut the hen into 8 large pieces. Do not let him remove any fat from this chicken. You will remove excess fat later, but the soup has to cook with the fat for flavor.

Put the chicken feet in a bowl, cover them with boiling water, and let them sit in the boiling water for at least 15 minutes. Then plunge them into ice water. This will make them easier to peel. With a sharp knife, peel off the entire outer layer of tough yellow skin.

In another bowl, pour more boiling water over the chicken parts. Then scrape the skin with a small sharp knife to remove any pinfeathers still sticking to the skin and any dirt that adheres to the fatty skin from the processing of the chicken. Soaking and scraping the skin result in a much cleaner broth and almost no scum rising to the surface of the soup to be skimmed away during cooking.

COOKING

Add the cleaned chicken parts and feet to the pot, including the neck, the neck skin, and the gizzard but not the liver because it will make the soup taste bitter. Add 3 quarts (12 cups) boiling water to the pot, and cook, uncovered, over highest heat until the water comes to a boil again. Reduce heat slightly, and let the chicken cook for about 5 minutes, skimming away any gray gook that rises to the surface. When the broth seems to be clear, add all other ingredients, cover the pot, and reduce the heat so that the liquid simmers. Allow contents to simmer for 2 ½ hours. It is not necessary to peek into the pot very often once you have adjusted the heat.

After 2 ½ hours turn off the heat. It doesn't hurt to let everything steep in the covered pot for another hour or so if you're not in a terrible rush. The soup will have tremendous body and flavor.

Remove the chicken and vegetables. Strain the soup back into the pot. If you want to remove most of the fat immediately from the top of the soup—you must leave a smidgen for color and flavor—pour the soup into a "souperstrainer," a plastic pitcher that pours from the bottom rather than the top. Otherwise put the pot of soup in the refrigerator to cool until the fat congeals on top. Then just lift most of the fat off with a spatula.

Remove the chicken meat from the bones. If your family doesn't like boiled chicken added to the soup, make chicken salad from it (see page 52). You can slice the cooked carrots and celery and add them to the soup when serving. When ready to serve, reheat the soup, taste, and adjust seasoning with salt. Serve over noodles or rice, with cooked carrots, celery, and chicken meat, if desired.

SERVING

You will end up with about 8 cups of certified Jewish Penicillin that will serve 3 hungry ethnics—or 8 others.

Mother Wonderful's

Favorite Boiled Chicken Re-creations and Side Dishes

My mother was a truly great cook, with an ability to experiment and grow. Here are some samples of her culinary legerdemain, turning the yuckiest ingredient on earth, boiled soup chicken, which no one in our household ate unless we were actually starving, into delicious entrées we all clamored for, plus a few of her special side dishes that she often served with them.

Tsuni's Knaidlach or Matzo Balls for Chicken Soup

INGREDIENTS

2 tablespoons rendered chicken fat
  (schmaltz) or peanut oil
  (chicken fat tastes better)
2 large eggs, slightly beaten
½ cup matzo meal
½ to 1 teaspoon salt
2 tablespoons club soda or seltzer (my
  mother's secret ingredient!)

PREPARATION

Mix the fat and eggs together with a
wire whisk in a bowl. Add the matzo
meal and salt slowly, blending in well
with the wire whisk. Add the club soda,
and whisk well again. Cover the bowl,
and place in refrigerator for at least 30
minutes. An hour is even better.

COOKING

Bring 2 quarts of salted water to a brisk
boil on high heat. Lower the heat, and
wait until the water is bubbling just
slightly. Divide the batter into 12 equal
parts, and roll them into balls. Drop the
balls in water. Cover the pot, and let it
simmer for about 40 minutes. Don't look
into the pot every 5 minutes. The matzo
balls will not fly away. Look into the pot
after 40 minutes. If the matzo balls have
risen to the surface, they are done. If
they haven't, throw them out and try
again, unless you like dumplings that
have the texture and consistency of can-
nonballs.

Remove the cooked matzo balls, and
add them to soup. Reheat to serve.

SERVING

Two matzo balls will more than suffice
per serving of soup. They can also be
used as vegetarian dumplings added to
brisket gravy or tomato sauce.

Tsuni's Rebaked Boiled Chicken

This is another disguise for boiled soup chicken that my mother's son-in-law adores. But then again he adores almost everything edible. The only two dishes he refuses to eat or even consider eating are stewed spleen and fricasseed lung. Lucky for me he draws a line somewhere.

INGREDIENTS

Boiled chicken from soup
Salt
Pepper
Garlic powder
Paprika
Olive oil

Preheat oven to 450 degrees F.

PREPARATION & COOKING

Place drained boiled soup chicken in a baking pan, skin side up. Sprinkle with salt, pepper, garlic powder, and paprika. Bake on the top shelf of the oven for 8 minutes, or until it browns slightly. Then sprinkle with olive oil, and bake for 2 minutes more, or until the chicken can pass for roasted chicken.

VARIATION

A variation on this is to cut 2 pounds of unpeeled red bliss potatoes, 1 bunch of unpeeled carrots, and 2 peeled onions into quarters. Place them in a baking pan, sprinkle them with 2 tablespoons olive oil, salt, and fresh snipped rosemary, and bake them at 450 degrees for 20 minutes. Then add the chicken, and proceed as above.

Tsuni's Fake Tuna Fish Salad

As a child I was considered a juvenile Jewish anorectic, which meant I could live off my own fat for only seventeen weeks (see photo). "The child eats nothing!" was the constant lament of my mother and grandmother because I didn't like what was considered "normal" food. They spent countless hours making dishes I <u>would</u> eat. This is one of them. I didn't eat "normal" chicken salad, but I loved tuna fish salad, so my mother concocted a chicken salad that could pass as tuna fish salad. Here it is.

INGREDIENTS

2 cups finely chopped or shredded skinless,
   boneless boiled soup chicken
½ cup chopped fennel or celery
½ cup thinly sliced scallions
1 tablespoon $25 bottle balsamic vinegar (the greatest!)
   or lime juice
6 tablespoons mayonnaise
2 pinches of cayenne pepper or a few drops of chili oil
½ jar small capers, drained

PREPARATION

Mix all the ingredients together with a fork as if you were making tuna fish salad. Let the mixture sit in the refrigerator for a few hours to mellow. This salad keeps very well. You can add two chopped hard-boiled eggs if desired. My mother always added hard-boiled egg, which she also added to genuine tuna fish salad, to disguise this chicken salad even more.

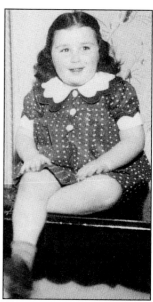

The child who "ate nothing!"

Tsuni's Chicken Salad Oriental

My mother grew into a more sophisticated epicure by experimenting with ingredients she found in my house. This chicken salad is an example of the kind of dish she created after I married and is the one that her son-in-law loves.

INGREDIENTS

4 cups (or more) leftover skinless and boneless boiled soup chicken, cut into cubes or just shredded if the chicken has been simmered to smithereens

1 cup thinly sliced fennel

1 cup thinly sliced scallions, including 1 inch of green tops

1½ cups julienned daikon radish or ordinary turnip

1 cup thinly sliced red pepper

DRESSING

1 cup mayonnaise (if you make your own, include 6 tablespoons sesame oil in your ingredients)

2 tablespoons raspberry or cider vinegar

2 tablespoons low-salt soy sauce

1 tablespoon green peppercorn or Dijon mustard

2 teaspoons sugar

1 teaspoon pressed elephant garlic or ½ teaspoon pressed garlic ordinaire

1 teaspoon grated fresh ginger

1 teaspoon lime juice

½ teaspoon ground white pepper

¼ teaspoon five-spice powder

PREPARATION

Toss the chicken, fennel, scallions, daikon radish, and pepper. Blend the mayonnaise and all the other dressing ingredients with a wire whisk. Toss together the dressing and all other ingredients. Refrigerate until ready to serve. If you can't find daikon radish, try chunks of bok choy or Chinese celery. You can experiment with the vegetables, but not with the dressing. That should always be the same.

Tsuni's Chicken Croquettes

My mother's basic chicken croquette recipe featured gently sautéed rather than deep-fried patties. Dill and Tabasco, if you want to add them, give the fixings a little bit more of a zing.

BASIC RECIPE

INGREDIENTS

6 scallions with 3 inches of green tops
1 slice white bread with crusts removed
8 ounces skinless and boneless boiled soup chicken
2 eggs
½ to 1 teaspoon salt
¼ teaspoon pepper
½ teaspoon garlic powder
1 tablespoon lime or lemon juice
1 teaspoon dried dill (optional)
8 drops of Tabasco (optional)
Oil or margarine for frying

PREPARATION & COOKING

Combine all the ingredients but the oil in a food processor until fine. Heat the oil over medium heat. Divide the chicken mush into ¼-cup servings, make each into a patty, and fry until golden brown on both sides. The croquettes keep well, and they will mellow and taste even better the following morning—that is, if anyone in your household lets them last that long.

MIDDLE EASTERN VARIATION

The variation has a slightly sweet yet savory Sephardic taste.

INGREDIENTS

6 scallions with 3 inches of green tops
1 slice white bread with crusts removed
8 ounces skinless and boneless boiled soup chicken
2 eggs
½ to 1 teaspoon salt
⅛ teaspoon nutmeg
¼ cup golden raisins
1 tablespoon dry vermouth
Oil for frying

PREPARATION & COOKING

Combine all the ingredients but the oil in a food processor until fine. Heat the oil over medium heat. Divide the chicken mush into ¼-cup servings, make each into a patty, and fry until golden brown on both sides. These also improve with age and refrigeration, etc., etc.

SERVING

Both can be served as is or with Almost Instant Tomato Sauce Mishmash, or as a replacement for chicken in Gumbo (see page 60).

Tsuni's Fried Liver Noodle Kugel

My mother created this unusual form of noodle kugel. Everybody loved it because the chicken livers came as a surprise treat. She either sliced it into wedges and served it as a side dish, or cut it into 1-inch squares and added to the hot chicken soup. She used margarine or oil because they are kosher, but butter can also be used by anyone who either does not observe Jewish dietary laws, or has cholesterol levels that have dipped dangerously low.

NOODLE INGREDIENTS

½ teaspoon salt
1 teaspoon bland blended oil
½ pound very fine egg noodles

TO PRECOOK THE NOODLES

Cook the noodles as directed on the package, but add salt to the water and oil to prevent the noodles from sticking together. Be careful not to overcook the noodles. Drain them immediately under cold water to stop the cooking, and reserve.

LIVER INGREDIENTS

2 tablespoons margarine or bland blended oil
4 scallions, including three inches of green tops, sliced into thin, elongated ovals
4 chicken livers cut into quarters (or ¼ pound of calves liver cut into 1½-inch chunks). The best livers come from free-range chickens, if you can get some extras. You know the drill. Tell the butcher to steal some from somebody else's hen.

TO PRECOOK THE LIVERS

Heat margarine or oil, add scallions, and sauté over medium heat until the scallions are soft but not brown. Then add the chunks of liver and sauté until the liver is medium-well done. Remove from heat and let cool. Cut livers into a ¼–½ inch dice, and reserve.

THE FINAL STEPS

4 eggs
1 teaspoon salt
⅛ teaspoon pepper
½ teaspoon garlic powder
5 tablespoons margarine or bland blended oil

COOKING

Add cooked scallions and livers to the reserved cooked noodles. Beat eggs with salt, pepper, and garlic powder. Pour into the liver-noodle base and mix well. Heat three tablespoons of oil or margarine over medium heat in a nonstick 10-inch skillet with straight sides. Spoon the noodle mixture into the pan and cook over medium heat for 10 minutes or until the bottom of the noodle mass is set and golden brown. Put a plate over the pan and turn the kugel over. Heat the remaining margarine or oil, then fry the uncooked side of the noodle kugel for 10 minutes more over medium heat or until it is also golden brown.

Remove from pan and blot excess oil with paper towels.

Tsuni's White Squash Latkes

As a child I didn't like potato pancakes. Why? Pure perversity, because Tsuni's were delicious. She concocted this dish for me from white pattypan squash. I loved it. So did everyone else. I had to fight them off to get enough for myself.

INGREDIENTS

½ pound white squash, quartered, peeled, and seeded
4 scallions with 3 inches of green tops
1 large egg
½ teaspoon baking powder
¼ teaspoon salt
⅛ teaspoon white pepper
2 tablespoons flour
Plain blended oil
Butter or margarine (optional)
Sour cream (optional)

PREPARATION & COOKING

Chop up the squash and scallions in a food processor. Add the egg, baking powder, salt, pepper, flour, and blend until smooth.

Heat the oil over medium heat. Immediately drop the squash mixture by tablespoonful in the hot oil. You have to cook this as soon as it's blended; otherwise the batter gets watery.

Fry for 1½ to 2 minutes on each side. Drain on paper towels.

SERVING

Keep warm in a double boiler. These pancakes swell because of the baking powder; then they sink. My mother preferred them when they'd sunk, so she put them in a double boiler and dressed them with dabs of butter or margarine for better flavor. They are wonderful with sour cream.

Tsuni's Potato Latkes

INGREDIENTS

2 large eggs
¼ cup grated onions
¾ teaspoon salt
¼ teaspoon white pepper
2 tablespoons bread crumbs or matzo meal
1 teaspoon lemon juice
¼ teaspoon dried thyme
1 ½ large red bliss potatoes, peeled and grated
½ cup of oil, butter, or (gasp!) schmaltz (rendered chicken fat)

PREPARATION & COOKING

Beat the eggs. Add the onions, salt, pepper, crumbs, lemon juice, and thyme. Grate the potatoes on a medium fine grater. Squeeze in a towel to remove as much water as possible. Add to the egg mixture.

Heat half the oil in a frying pan, and drop the potato mixture into it by the tablespoonful, adding oil as required. Fry over medium heat until browned on both sides. Drain in a paper bag or paper towels, and keep warm in oven until all are fried.

Tsuni's Almost Instant Tomato Sauce Mishmash, or Gumbo

Tsuni used to make tomato sauce by cooking it for several hours, until she determined that the only reason to cook the sauce for such a long time was to give the liquid in it a chance to boil off. If she controlled the amount of liquid she added, it didn't need to simmer for so long.

INGREDIENTS

2 tablespoons soy oil
1 tablespoon sesame oil
1½ teaspoons kosher salt
¼ teaspoon pepper
3 red peppers, cut into slices 1½ inches long by ¼ inch wide
1 bunch scallions, sliced into ¼-inch rounds
1 medium sweet onion, peeled, cut in half, and sliced thin
1 fennel bulb, cut into quarters, core removed, and sliced thin
1 clove elephant garlic, cut in half and sliced very thin
1 carrot, cut into 2-inch-long juliennes
3 cans stewed tomatoes, drained
1 can tomato sauce
⅓ cup Madeira, sweet Marsala, or sherry
1 tablespoon low-salt soy sauce
¼ teaspoon chili oil
¼ teaspoon five-spice powder
½ teaspoon sugar

COOKING

Heat the oils. Add the salt and pepper; then sauté the vegetables and garlic for 15 minutes over medium heat. Add all the other ingredients one by one. Simmer for 5 minutes, and it's ready to serve.

SERVING

It can be served hot over pasta or rice, used as a base to which sausage or ground meat is added, or served cold as a condiment with meat, fish, or chicken.

Tsuni's Faux Gumbo

INGREDIENTS

1 batch Almost Instant Tomato Sauce Mishmash
Skinless and boneless boiled soup chicken
1 teaspoon cumin
Okra

COOKING

To the Almost Instant Tomato Sauce add ½ pound sliced, frozen, or fresh okra to the initial vegetable sauté. Add chicken or chicken croquettes and cumin, and heat through.

Tsuni's Zucchini Spaghetti

PREPARATION & COOKING

On a mandolin, slice the nonseeded portions of a large, firm unpeeled 8-inch zucchini into strands that resemble spaghetti by running the zucchini through the ⅛-inch shoestring julienne cutters and a thinly set cutting blade at the same time. This can also be done with a sharp knife and steady hands. The spaghetti has a green cast, and people will think you're serving spinach pasta, but zucchini spaghetti contains 84 calories a pound, and pasta contains 100 calories per ounce.

Blanch the zucchini strands in boiling salted water for no more than 1 minute, drain, and toss with Almost Instant Tomato Sauce (see page 60).

About the Author

At forty-one, Myra Chanin was a depressed housewife whose marriage looked doomed. After ten years of not exactly wedded bliss, she had raised her level of self-esteem and no longer agreed that her husband, Alvin, that long-suffering saint, was supermarvy and she was a lucky woman to have the honor of waiting on him. Thus began a saga of midlife blossoming that inspires all who hear it.

Myra believed baking was the only skill she possessed that would supply her with enough income to hire a really heartless divorce lawyer. She went into the cheesecake business as Mother Wonderful, her cakes won awards, and her marriage stabilized as soon as Alvin realized that change might be less debilitating for him than losing half his assets.

Myra gave away her cheesecake business to attempt her heart's desire, writing humor. In 1980 her first book, *The Secret Life of Mother Wonderful*, was published. In it she described her attempts to change Alvin into Rhett Butler, a task only slightly less difficult than emptying the Atlantic Ocean into the Pacific Ocean with the aid of a sieve.

But cheesecake would not be denied, and soon her second book, *Mother Wonderful's Cheesecakes and Other Goodies*, appeared in bookstores to great acclaim. Did cheesecake save her marriage? It didn't hurt. She and Alvin are billing and cooing after thirty years. Their son, Steven, is a wonderful young man—everything Alvin would have been if he'd only had Myra as his mother.

Presently Chanin can be heard as the culinary commentator for *Artbeat*, the weekly National Public Radio magazine on arts in America.

Myra Chanin